Color Shit!
Swear Word Coloring Book Belongs To

_____

Copyright © 2022 Little Coloring
All rights reserved. No part of this publication may be reproduced, distributed, or transmitted in any form or by any means, including photocopying, recording, or other electronic or mechanical methods, without the prior written permission of the publisher.

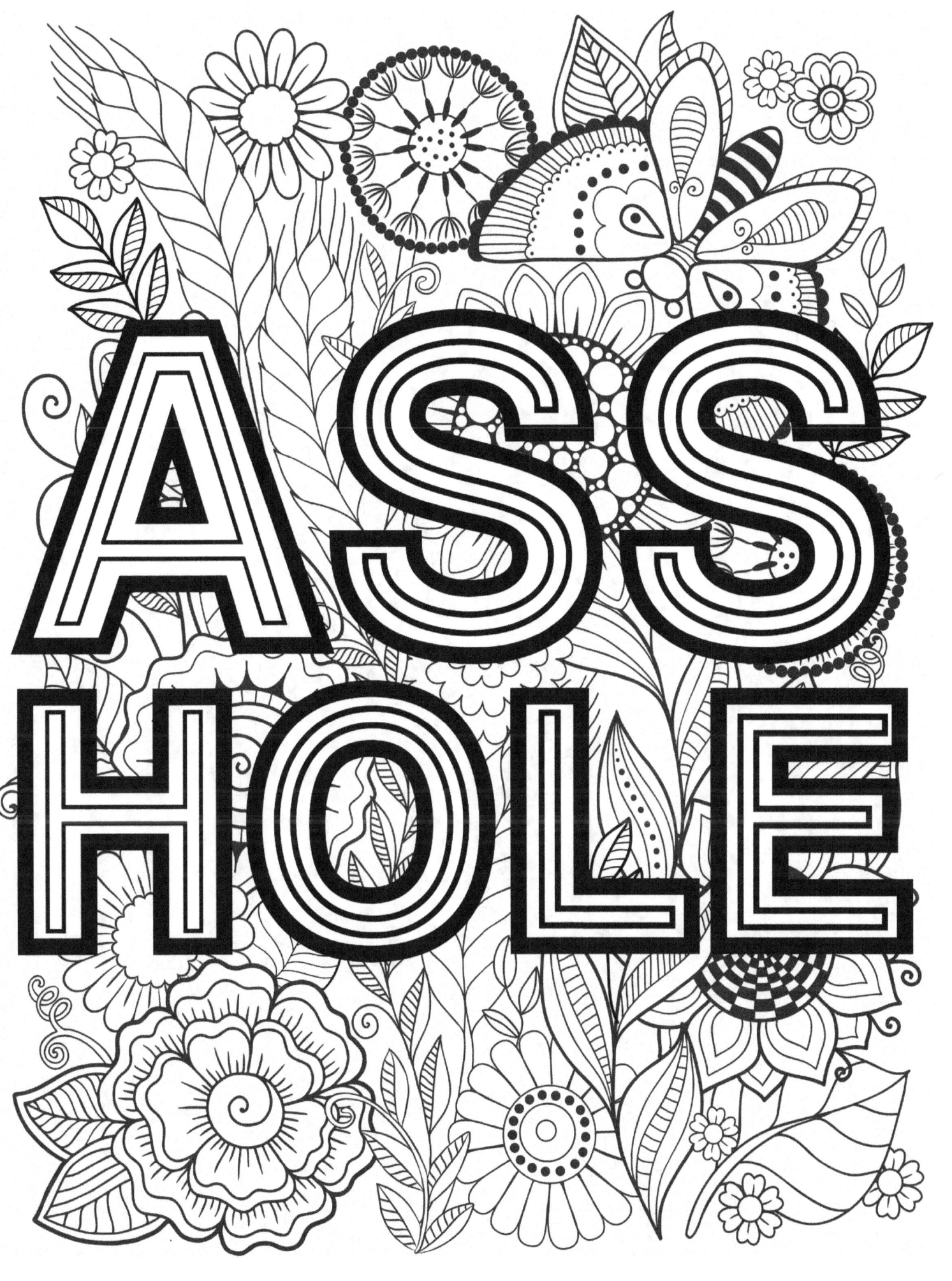

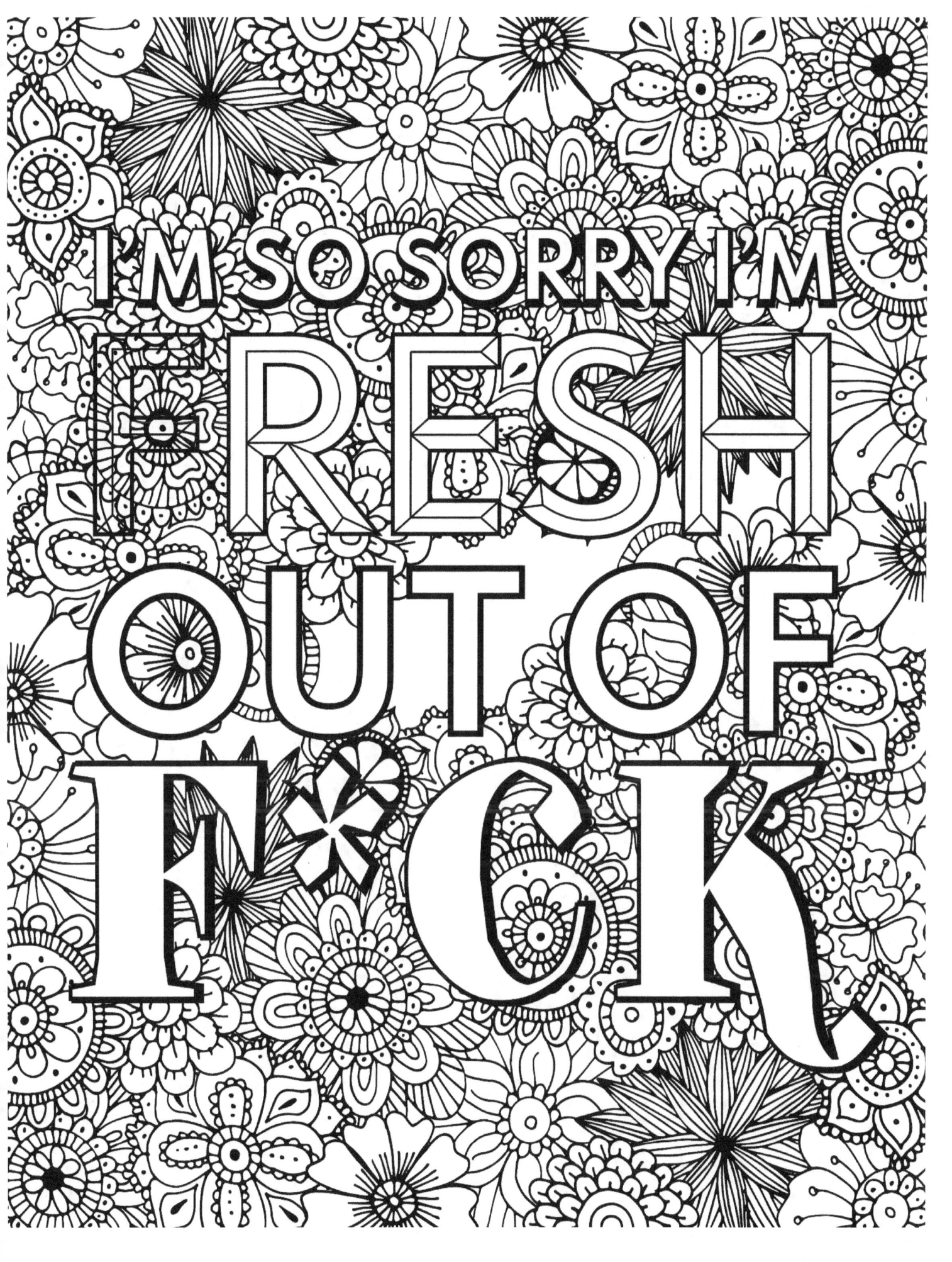

www.ingramcontent.com/pod-product-compliance
Lightning Source LLC
Chambersburg PA
CBHW082115220526
45472CB00009B/2184